ALPHABEASTS

DICK KING-SMITH'S
ALPHABEASTS

illustrated by
QUENTIN BLAKE

Macmillan Publishing Company
New York

Maxwell Macmillan International
New York   Oxford   Singapore   Sydney

First American Edition 1992

Macmillan Publishing Company is part of the
Maxwell Communication Group of Companies.

Macmillan Publishing Company
866 Third Avenue
New York, NY 10022

Originally published in Great Britain by
Victor Gollancz Ltd., London, in 1990.

Printed in Singapore

10   9   8   7   6   5   4   3   2   1

Library of Congress Cataloging-in-Publication Data is available.

ISBN 0-02-750720-3

FOR MYRLE
—DK-S

FOR JOHN NORRIS WOOD
—QB

They say the dodo's gone for good.
For good? Why, what a thing to say
When such a host of animals
No longer sees the light of day.

The quagga and the thylacine,
The great auk and the nandi bear,
The sea mink and the bulldog rat—
You will not find them anywhere.

And oh, so many more besides
Are simply names whose day has passed,
Who've shot their bolt and had their chips
And run their course and breathed their last.

Extinction! It's a fearful thought
So now's the time to use our powers
To save the creatures of the world—
The world that's theirs as much as ours.

A stands for ANACONDA, who, however, will not stand
For interfering foreigners intruding on his land.
If he can eat explorers who accost him in Brazil,
As is the Anaconda's wont, the Anaconda will.

The nose of Long-nosed BANDICOOT
Is longer (as you might have thought)
Than that of Short-nosed Bandicoot,
Which (as you might have guessed) is short.

In short, you cannot doubt for long
Which is which kind of Bandicoot;
You find if you are right or wrong
By simply measuring its snoot.

C

The CIVETS reside in the coconut palms
(Where the locals hang jars to make toddy).
When the locals go home from their coconut farms,
Then the Civets come out in a body.
They imbibe as the sun settles over Malay,
They continue long after it's sunk,
And though some of the Civets can pack it away,
Quite a lit of the Covets get drunk.

D

The DUGONG, or sea cow, is rocked by the motion
Of gentle warm waves in the Indian Ocean,
And clasps to her horrible breast with one flipper
The sickening face of her hideous nipper.

Seen thus in an anthropomorphic position,
The Dugong gives rise to the sailors' tradition
Of beautiful mermaids. A fair compensation
For being the ugliest beast in creation.

E

The American ᴇʟᴋ—also known as the wapiti—
Runs through the maple woods, clippety-cloppety.
Favored with feet of remarkable property,
Wapitis never have need of chiropody.

There are five hundred sorts of FLEAS,
(Just forty-six in Britain),
Which goes to show variety's
The spice of being bitten.

The GECKO has adhesive toes,
Straight up the wall the Gecko goes.
And then—and this is most appealing—
The Gecko walks across the ceiling!

Foolhardy is the one who tries
This topsy-turvy exercise.
To sudden death you will be fated—
The Gecko can't be imitated.

H

To the sound of a string of hysterical moans,
Like a lunatic's laugh, it is said,
The horrid HYENA will crack up your bones
(But he only does this if you're dead).

I

High on Caucasian crags and convexities,
Cliffs and crevasses and cols, and complexities
Where the most skilled mountaineers, if they were to go
Climbing, would certainly suffer from vertigo,
Heavy-horned IBEX, his yellow eyes cynical,
Caprioles coolly from peak on to pinnacle,
Confident both of the muscles that *he* flexes
And the effects of an Ibex's reflexes.

J

The JAGUAR lies secretly in trees,
Whence with abandon and gymnastic ease
It drops upon you as you walk below,
And breaks your neck with one effective blow.

The Amazonian, on his native plot,
Refers to them as "tigers," which they're not.
The difference, as you expire like this,
Must be, however, pure hypothesis.

K

To call a small Australian bird
(The size a common pigeon is)
A "laughing jackass," seems absurd
To learned aborigines.

They therefore, you'll be glad to hear,
With logic far more thorough
Make use of onomatopoeia,
And call it KOOKABURRA.

L

Do not alarm a LLAMA,
It really is unwise
(As every Llama farmer
Must quickly recognise).

A most unpleasant drama
Unfolds, and he who tries
Should wear a suit of armor,
Or risk a sharp surprise.

No creature could be calmer
(Or so you might surmise),
But if you harm a Llama,
It spits right in your eyes.

M

The Praying MANTIS seems to be
Intent on its devotions,
And yet its intellect is free
Of all religious notions.

The Mantis male thinks, in a daze
Of love, "I'll court and win her!"
But when he has, the female preys—
She snaps him up for dinner.

N

The NIGHTJAR utters whirring notes,
And also is reputed
To suck the milk from sleeping goats.
(They, I am sure, refute it—
Having too many kids, you see,
To stand for such a liberty.)

O

The ORIBI's an antelope
That lives in Abyssinia.
It couldn't be much smaller
And it couldn't be much skinnier.

It couldn't be much smaller
And I couldn't much more sorry be,
But that's my total knowledge
Of the Abyssinian Oribi.

The PORCUPINES gnaw trees at night,
Whose bark is worsened by their bite,
And, arrogantly lurching round,
Emit a curious mumbling sound.

The passing predator construes
This note as menace and abuse,
And shuns, to noise of rattling spines,
Decorticating Porcupines.

Q

All gourmets care for QUAIL a lot—
From Delaware to Delhi.
Some swear they must be eaten hot,
Some cold in aspic jelly.

R

Now you know and I know
The African RHINO
Is truculent to a degree.

But I know (do you know?)
The Rhino will do no
One harm if you leave the thing be.

They pulverize passers
Who treat them, alas, as
A suitable butt for a prank.

So do not incite one
Or offer to fight one,
Unless you are driving a tank.

S

Now the SLOTH is both unhurried
And affects a fearful frown.
This is not because he's worried
But because he's upside down.

If the passerby inverts him,
It is patent, in a while,
That the strange position hurts him,
For the Sloth begins to smile.

The Common Snapping TURTLE likes to lie
In wait beneath the surface of a pool.
An unsuspecting duck that paddles by
Will vanish in a flash, unlucky fool.

Beware the Common Snapping Turtle's snap,
And do not swim, but stay upon the land.
Though fingers satisfy a little chap,
The larger ones prefer to take your hand.

UPUPA EPOPS is the name
Of a tedious bird called the hoopoe.
His song it is always the same—
"Poo-poo-poo, poo-poo-poo, poo-poo-*poo*-poo."

And this is a matter worth knowing
Concerning Upupa Epops.
You'll finish up glad when he's going.
And happier still when he stops.

V

The plains of Argentina
Are honeycombed with cells
Wherein the fat VISCACHA
Gregariously dwells.

The proud and swarthy gaucho
Hightails it out of town,
And stumbles on these burrows,
And falling, breaks his crown.

The priest commends the swarthy gaucho's soul.
The fat Viscacha digs another hole.

The Tasmanian WOMBAT is grizzly gray
And lies in the sunshine the whole of the day.
How nice to retire from the unequal combat
And copy the floppy Tasmanian Wombat.

The X-RAY FISH is very very small
And has no kind of privacy at all.
Though it may wish and wish you couldn't do it,
The fact remains that you can see right through it,
And ichthyologists—no ifs or buts—
Are all agreed, "The little chap's got guts!"

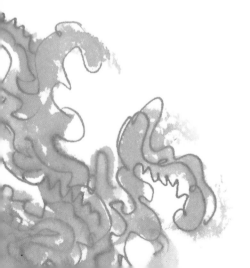

Y

In Tibet there's a species of YAK
Which is so unbelievably hairy

That you can't tell the front from the back,
So the traveler has to be wary

When he rides it, to face the right way.
Otherwise he'll go backwards all day.

Z

The ZAMBRA's a bison of old Lithuania
Which used to be nearly as common as lice on
A pig, until hunters developed a mania
For shooting the old Lithuanian bison.

The tragic conclusion (and so much the worse) is
The Zambra is finished . . .

And so are these verses.